25 Principles of Strategy

Title: 25 Principles of Strategy

I01?0321

Genre: Non-Fiction
Desc: Learn the 25 principles of strategy and adapt them in your everyday life.
Author: Kambiz Mostofizadeh
Publisher: Mikazuki Publishing House
ISBN-13: 978-1-942825-12-8
Date Published: August 2016

Copyright 2016 by Kambiz Mostofizadeh. All Rights Reserved.
No portion of this work may be copied, reproduced, printed, or scanned without the express written approval of the publisher.
The views represented in this work do not necessarily represent the views of the publisher.

25 Principles of Strategy

TABLE OF CONTENTS

25 Principles of Strategy

TOP STRATEGISTS OF ALL TIME

(In No Particular Order)

1. **Sun Tzu**

   Famous Chinese General that wrote the key treatise on military strategy. Advocated using military strategy to win without fighting.

2. **Carl Von Clausewitz**

   Famous European strategist that introduced Eastern military strategy to the West.

3. **Cyrus the Great**

   Famous Iranian leader that conquered $3/4^{th}$ of the known world using diplomacy and advanced military techniques.

25 Principles of Strategy

25 Principles of Strategy

4. Napoleon Bonaparte

French General and leader that pioneered the use of flanking techniques and maneuvering on the battlefield to defeat superiorly numbered forces.

5. Machiavelli

Italian strategist that advocated the use of intrigue and subterfuge to achieve political gains.

6. Miyamoto Musashi

Japanese swordsman and strategist famous for never losing in competition.

7. Salman Farsi

Iranian strategist that gave advice to Muslim armies, helping them defeat their enemies.

25 Principles of Strategy

8. Erwin Rommel

German World War II General famous for defeating superior forces using maneuvering and rapid deployment.

9. Toyotomi Hideyoshi

Japanese leader that united Japan using diplomacy and negotiation rather than violence.

10. Cao Cao

Chinese General and strategist famous for defeating the Yellow Turbans and uniting northern China.

11. General Suren

Parthian (Iranian) strategist that defeated 44,000 Romans (in modern day Turkey) using advanced military strategy.

25 Principles of Strategy

WHAT ABOUT STRATEGY?

Carl Von Clausewitz stated in his multi-volume book series titled "On War" that "the theory of the Grande Guerre, or Strategy, as it is called, is beset with extraordinary difficulties, and we may affirm that very few men have clear conceptions of the separate subjects, that is, conceptions carried up to their full logical conclusions. In real action most men are guided merely by the tact of judgment which hits the object more or less accurately, according as they possess more or less genius." Chang Yu stated in the Art of War that "while the main laws of strategy can be stated clearly enough for the benefit of all and sundry, you must be guided by the actions of the enemy in attempting to secure a favorable position in actual warfare." Strategy, as a means to the end which is victory, has to be pragmatic, realistic, and based on the actual

25 Principles of Strategy

Carl Von Clausewitz

conditions that exist. Machiavelli said "For supposing two of your powerful neighbors come to blows, it must either be that you have, or have not, reason to fear the one who comes off victorious. In either case it will always be

25 Principles of Strategy

well for you to declare yourself, and join in frankly with one side or other.

Sun Tzu

25 Principles of Strategy

For should you fail to do so you are certain, in the former of the cases put, to become the prey of the victor to the satisfaction and delight of the vanquished, and no reason or circumstance that you may plead will avail to shield or shelter you; for the victor dislikes doubtful friends, and such as will not help him at a pinch; and the vanquished will have nothing to say to you, since you would not share his fortunes sword in hand."

Strategy is the means by which you achieve victory.

A strategist should have the following attributes:

- Understanding of the environment they are operating in.

- Adaptability to chaos and surprise

- Able to see and lead change

- Able to get things done by building trust

25 Principles of Strategy

- Able to be ethical

- Able to think critically and strategically

According to the Defense Technical Information Center document titled "Sound Decision" from 1936, "Actually, while tactical considerations may predominate during battle, their influence is not confined to the immediate presence of the enemy. Tactical dispositions are frequently adopted for convenience, for time saving, or for other reasons, long before entry into the immediate presence of the enemy. Nor do strategical considerations end when battle is joined. Tactics, unguided by strategy, might blindly make sacrifices merely to remain victor on a field of struggle. But strategy looks beyond, in order to make the gains or tactics accord with the strategic aim. Strategy and tactics are inseparable. It is thus the duty of

25 Principles of Strategy

tactics to ensure that its results are appropriate to the strategic aim, and the duty of strategy to place at the disposal of tactics the power appropriate to the results demanded. The latter consideration imposes upon strategy the requirement that the prescribed aim be possible of attainment with the power that can be made available. Consequently, while the attainment of the aims of strategy generally depends upon the results gained by tactics, strategy is initially responsible for the success of tactics. It is therefore in the province of strategy to ensure that the attainment of tactical objectives furthers, exclusively, the aims of strategy, and also that the tactical struggle be initiated under conditions favorable for the attainment of the designated objectives."

25 Principles of Strategy

Cyrus the Great

PRINCIPLE OF AUDACITY

The Principle of Audacity states that audacity will allow you to overcome obstacles. Carl Von Clausewitz was a major proponent of this

25 Principles of Strategy

principle of strategy. Von Clausewitz believed that audacity will allow a leader to be able to overcome any obstacles put before him because of his audacity. Von Clausewitz believed that being timid was a sign of weakness and that audacity showed strength. Looking at the famous Chinese strategist Sun Tzu, he believed that it is better to show weakness during strength and to show strength during weakness. Von Clausewitz was arguing audacity could be the key defining factor between winning and losing. In strategy, it is better to be on the offensive than to rather play a purely defensive game. You can avoid a fast defeat by playing purely defensively but that does not allow you to win. Being on the offensive allows you to win. In order to be on the offensive, you must have audacity. Von Clausewitz also stated that "energy in forced

25 Principles of Strategy

marches, boldness in sudden attacks, the intensified activity which great souls acquire in the moment of danger, these are the grounds of such victories; and what have these to do with the ability to make an exact calculation of two such simple things as time and space?" Great things could be accomplished if you have courage and boldness in the face of seemingly impossible odds. The greater the odds are against you, the more audacity is needed to push forward during uncertain times. You cannot accomplish anything that would be considered great if you have a defeatist attitude or a timid attitude. Your attitude should be bold and courageous in order for you to be able to achieve great things. No one has propelled themselves forward in life or in a situation by expressing a timid attitude. Being bold is not the same as not being cautious. You should be cautious but you should also be

25 Principles of Strategy

bold enough to seize opportunities as they present themselves. In many military conflicts throughout history, there have been numerous examples of boldness and audacity leading to a winning situation in what seemed to be a sure defeat. The Principle of Audacity, as the 1st principle, can be the defining factor between winning and losing.

PRINCIPLE OF RESERVATION

The Principle of Reservation is the 2nd principle of the 25 Principles of Strategy. The Principle of Reservation states that you should not use all of your strength when the situation does not demand it. Sun Tzu states in the Art of War that "Now, when your weapons are dulled, your ardor damped, your strength exhausted and your treasure spent, other chieftains will spring up to take advantage of your extremity. Then no man, however wise, will be able to avert the

25 Principles of Strategy

consequences that must ensue." Sun Tzu is stating that if you spend everything you have attempting to achieve a possibly unreachable goal, you will not only lose everything you have, but your enemies, foes, and competitors are the ones that will become enriched by your destitute state. Saving resources and using them wisely is the essence of the Principle of Reservation. Not all goals can be reached and not all mountains can be climbed. By conserving resources and building a reserve, you will be safe and secure during times of economic uncertainty. By wasting your reserves, you are cutting away your strength. Maintaining and building up reserves will allow you to persevere under difficult conditions. If you lose all your resources, you will be powerless and weak. If you lose all your resources, it will take longer for you to find your way back to the position from which you

25 Principles of Strategy

started. The Principle of Reservation argues for thrift in action and minimal resources applied to achieve the required task. If you apply your resources economically and sparingly, you will be able to continue moving forward until your task or goal is completed. If you waste resources, then you will find yourself in a difficult situation that may result in you having to abandon your current gains in order to save yourself.

PRINCIPLE OF NON-ENGAGEMENT

The principle of Non-Engagement is the 3rd principle of the 25 Principles of Strategy and it teaches that not all conflicts are won by fighting. Sun Tzu said "Hence to fight and conquer in all your battles is not supreme excellence. Supreme excellence consists in breaking the enemy's resistance without fighting." Sun Tzu was referring to the 3rd

25 Principles of Strategy

principle of the 25 Principles of Strategy and that is the Principle of Non-Engagement. In the multiple military invasions of Scotland by King Edward I of England, the Scottish Armies decided on multiple occasions to avoid engaging militarily the English forces. The English forces wasted precious resources, lost men to diseases, lost horses, lost gold (money), lost time, and lost face, attempting to engage the Scottish who had decided not to engage the invaders. By simply not engaging, the English were now at a

serious disadvantage and were losing resources the longer the invasion continued. The Scottish simply hid for short or long periods of time, causing the English forces to waste precious resources. In addition, part of the Scottish stratagem of laying siege included using ladders to climb the walls of the English castle silently and taking the castle without

25 Principles of Strategy

killing a single person. All battles do not depend on military might as many battles are decided by the strength of the mind rather than the strength of the weapon. Sun Tzu was stating that there are ways to win that do not involve having to militarily face your opponent. The Principle of Non-Engagement teaches that winning or losing is not dependent on fighting. Every question does not require an answer and every challenge does not require a challenger. The Principle of Non-Engagement teaches that by simply not-engaging the situation, the opponent will be forced to waste away resources, giving you a natural and obvious advantage.

25 Principles of Strategy

PRINCIPLE OF INTEGRATION

The 4th Principle of the 25 Principles of Strategy states that opponents can be integrated rather than competed with. The Persian Empire under Cyrus the Great integrated entire areas in to it without having to resort to bloodshed and violence. Using the Principle of Integration, foes were given rewards for being integrated creating the largest empire the world has witnessed. How was it achieved? Xenophon stated that "The Persian Empire was divided into not less than twenty provinces, each governed by a satrap appointed by the king and holding office at his pleasure. These satraps had courts, palaces, gardens, and lived in royal fashion. They collected the revenues, exercised the power of life and death, and were veritable tyrants, subject only to the great tyrant himself, called the great king. To secure their loyalty, he sent

25 Principles of Strategy

down to each province a commander of the royal forces and a secretary who was eyes and ears to the king, keeping him informed on all important matters. Later, the command of these troops was transferred to the satraps, and thus their power was greatly augmented." IBM is a perfect example of the Principle of Integration. By cooperating rather than competing, it is able to integrate companies in to its fold, creating more value for all that are aligned with it. Cooperation and integration creates strength by unity and acts a force multiplier, giving you an advantage that could not be acquired by competition. Competition can weaken you through the loss of resources but integration or cooperation can empower you and strengthen you. Competition is in many cases, counter-productive and weakens you. Sun Tzu said in the Art of War that "There is no instance of a nation having benefitted

25 Principles of Strategy

from prolonged warfare". Continuous competition is prolonged warfare while cooperation/integration can be considered established interdependent trade networks.

PRINCIPLE OF CONCENTRATION

The 5th Principle of the 25 Principles of Strategy states that in order for your actions to be effective, your resources have to be concentrated and focused. Resources are finite and are limited. You cannot be assured of success in an opportunity or situation if you divide your resources. Unity of resources allows for and creates success. If you "spread yourself too thin" by attempting to do tasks that are un-related to the main goal, this will sap your resources and weaken your strength. The Principle of Concentration calls for focus and concentration on the task or goal. This means that anything that is un-related to achieving the

25 Principles of Strategy

task or goal should be shunned or discarded. Because everyone is in a state of competition over the same resources, small actions towards your goal may only yield small results. By focusing all your resources towards achieving a goal, your chances of achieving that goal increase substantially. All opportunities, however enticing, cannot be pursued. Time as a resource, should be concentrated as much as financial resources are. Attempting to complete multiple tasks un-related to your main goal will create lost time, lost resources, and will sap your energy. By completely and totally concentrating all of your available time and resources towards the completion of your goal, the probability that the goal will reach completion is high. But when you spread your resources to multiple channels or to multiple opportunities simultaneously, the return, if any, will be small and not worth the

25 Principles of Strategy

time spent obtaining it. The 5th Principle of the 25 Principles of Strategy teaches above all that winning or losing in a given situation will be decided by the amount of focus or concentration of your resources towards achieving the said task or goal.

"Never doubt. Never fear. Never overthink."
- Ninja mantra

PRINCIPLE OF FLANKING

The 6th Principle of the 25 Principles of Strategy states that flanking maneuvers can be the defining factor between victory and defeat. Flanking maneuvers are indirect tactics rather than direct. Sun Tzu said "Indirect tactics, efficiently applied, are inexhaustible as Heaven and Earth, unending as the flow of rivers and streams; like the sun and moon, they end but

25 Principles of Strategy

to begin anew; like the four seasons, they pass away to return once more." French Emperor Napoleon Bonaparte is perhaps the most famous proponent of this method. Napoleon was famous spending hours studying geographical and topographical maps of a future battlefield, searching for locations or areas that could yield an advantage. Napoleon was known to be an excellent Chess player that would wear out his opponents using multiple strategies. According to the 1864 book titled 'Strategy and Tactics', "It is not always by taking position in the direct path of an enemy that his advance is opposed, but sometimes points may be occupied on the flank with much advantage, so as to threaten his line of operations if he ventures to pass. If these flank positions can be held in force, the enemy must leave his direct route to attack them, for, unless he carries them, he runs the risk of being cut

25 Principles of Strategy

off from his base. He is thus compelled to fight on ground selected by his adversary, and prepared for his reception by fortification and any other means circumstances may permit." Napoleon's dedication to total mastery of strategy made his as formidable on the battlefield as he was on a Chess board. Napoleon lived and breathed strategy, which is the means to the end, and the end being victory. Napoleon mastered and pioneered the use of flanking maneuvers to defeat armies that were many times more powerful than his own. A flanking maneuver is an indirect maneuver that would be considered un-orthodox. Direct maneuvers would have not created an advantage on the battlefield for Napoleon, who was already at a disadvantage in many of his battles because of his lack of an exceedingly large army. The 6th Principle of the 25 Principles of Strategy states flanking

25 Principles of Strategy

Flank

Opponent

25 Principles of Strategy

can be the difference between winning and losing.

PRINCIPLE OF MORALE

The 7th Principle of the 25 Principles of Strategy states morale can be the defining factor between winning and losing. Morale has been defined as the confidence, enthusiasm, and discipline of an army. Morale was a main element that powered Napoleon's armies to success. By Napoleon empowering his troops with high morale, his troops were able to defeat their enemies in many military battles while being vastly outnumbered. Napoleon believed that a troop with a high morale can defeat a troop five times its own number. Napoleon used many forced marches in his campaign, forcing his armies to move great distances in short periods of time. It was only be maintaining a high morale that he was able to

25 Principles of Strategy

create the victories that he did. Retreats and setbacks lower morale and gains and progression raise the morale. The higher the morale, the greater the capability to achieve results that could not be accomplished by mediocre morale. United States General Patton was also a famous proponent of high morale and was known to have a common touch, spending his time speaking and occasionally joking with his subordinates. Patton, who successfully won many battles in Europe during World War II, used the high morale of his troops to allow him to achieve difficult military successes. An army that lacks heart to continue fighting because it has lost its will, is a weak and divided force. The more enthusiasm the troops have towards achieving the goal or task at hand, the higher the morale is, increasing the chance of winning.

25 Principles of Strategy

According to Machiavelli "But when he is with his army, and has many soldiers under his command, he must needs disregard the reproach of cruelty, for without such a reputation in its Captain, no army can be held together or kept under any kind of control. Among other things remarkable in Hannibal this has been noted, that having a very great army, made up of men of many different nations and brought to fight in a foreign country, no dissension ever arose among the soldiers themselves, nor any mutiny against their leader, either in his good or in his evil fortunes. This we can only ascribe to the transcendent cruelty, which, joined with numberless great qualities, rendered him at once venerable and terrible in the eyes of his soldiers; for without this reputation for cruelty these other virtues would not have produced the like results."

25 Principles of Strategy

There are many instances, such as setbacks, that can lead to lower morale. Morale, whether high or low, is transitory and not permanent. Morale can be raised by giving your supporters gifts and money. A higher morale means that your supporters or followers will be more willing to undertake difficult situations that they may not have previously undertaken. Therefore it is of the greatest importance to a leader to attempt to achieve. Having high morale may allow you to accomplish goals that may have may have seemed impossible. Having high morale may allow you to overcome obstacles that may have been insurmountable. The 7th Principle of the 25 Principles of Strategy can be the defining factor between winning or losing.

25 Principles of Strategy

PRINCIPLE OF SILENCE

The 8th Principle of the 25 Principles of Strategy states that your actions should be silent to your opponents, if you seek to ensure your success. Do major corporations announce where the parts were manufactured used in their assembled product? No they do not. They announce where the product was assembled. Do companies announce publicly that they are using customer service departments in foreign nations to handle their business accounts? No they do not. It is frankly no one's business how you achieve your success in business. Companies do their business as usual and ask you to adjust yourself to their policies, do they not? You do not owe anyone anything. If you maintain your silence about your actions, your competitors will be confused about what you are doing. The Principle of Silence argues for maintaining your silence in order that your

25 Principles of Strategy

opponents to be forced to speculate. If you are seeking to win rather than lose against your opponent, you have to maintain silence so that your plans are not copied. Silence is vital to your success because it hides the form and patterns of your actions. If your opponents discover what you're doing, then your plans will lose their efficacy and their effectiveness. The Principle of Silence argues for maintaining your silence by not announcing your plans. Your plans when announced, allow for mimicry and copy-cat type behavior. Of course you cannot execute public relations programs without the use of announcements, but the Principle of Silence when applied, would make the announcements in to informational notifications rather than veiled advertisements. Having more resources will not help you achieve victory if your opponents know of the 8th Principle of the 25 Principles of Strategy states

25 Principles of Strategy

that silence can be the defining factor between winning and losing because the absence of the news of your plans makes your opponents have to speculate.

"At night ears have to do the duty of eyes."
-Xenophon

PRINCIPLE OF OPPOSITES

The 9th Principle of the 25 Principles of Strategy states that opposite forces create opportunities for winning. In the Vietnam War, the United States Armed Forces used superior firepower, chemical weapons, advanced helicopters, fighter jets, and every resource at its disposal to fight a vastly inferior opponent. The Viet Kong moved anti-tank weapons on bicycles through steep mountain jungles, created entire cities under the ground that served as civilian and military bases, and executed textbook guerrilla warfare tactics to

25 Principles of Strategy

defeat the vastly superior American armed forces. The Viet Kong beat the United States Armed Forces by using the Principle of Opposites. By playing the opposite to the United States Armed Forces, the Viet Kong were able to achieve success and bring defeat to their opponent. The United States Army and Marines were conventional soldiers that were both highly trained and highly disciplined. Vietnam lowered the morale of the invading American soldiers because the enemy, the Viet Kong, fought a guerrilla warfare campaign that skillfully took apart the vastly superior American forces. By using the Principle of Opposites, the Viet Kong achieved success by fighting the High Technology American War Machine with the Low Technology Vietnamese War Machine. The Principle of Opposites is proven in warfare as much as it is proven in the public relations arena. The more you badmouth

25 Principles of Strategy

your opponent, the more famous your opponent becomes. In Public Relations it is common knowledge that there is no such thing as bad press. In many cases, individuals have become famous from bad press while the good press they generated did not have the same effect for them. This has been proven to be true time and time again. The 9th Principle of the 25 Principles of Strategy argues for playing the opposite to your opponent in order to create differentiation between you and them as well as to win against a stronger opponent. The Principle of Opposites can be the defining factor between winning and losing.

PRINCIPLE OF MOMENTUM

The 10th Principle of the 25 Principles of Strategy states that building and maintaining momentum can lead to winning. Momentum is built over time and through building support.

25 Principles of Strategy

Momentum that is built too quickly can dissipate just as fast. Momentum, for it to be effective, has to be built naturally over time. Many military battles have been won by weaker forces that had the advantage of momentum. In order to create momentum, there has to be supporters that will aid you in building momentum. Whether they are influencers or if they are decision-makers or stakeholders, momentum can be derived from creating support. It is easier to move a boulder with 5 people than it is alone. But once the boulder is moved, it will continue rolling and creating even greater momentum. The difficulty lies in the initial stage of moving the boulder.

"When he utilizes combined energy, his fighting men become as it were like unto rolling logs or stones. For it is the nature of a log or stone to

25 Principles of Strategy

remain motionless on level ground, and to
move when on a slope; if four-cornered,
to come to a standstill, but if round-shaped, to
go rolling down."
-Sun Tzu

Whether your goal or task is small or large, it
will be easier to create momentum and develop
it by working with others. Building momentum
is not dependent on creating any type of
hierarchal organization or clock-work like
synchronicity. Building momentum depends
you being able to align yourself with individuals
from whose relationship benefit will be created
that will allow you to derive support. The smart
and wise leader will put in time for building
important relationships that can allow support
to be generated. From this support, momentum
is created. However small the action of a
supporter for you, it is the sum of all the

25 Principles of Strategy

support that creates the momentum that propels you forward. The momentum is built up diligently and meticulously over time and it is harvested for your benefit when the timing is right for doing so. Many weaker and undermanned military forces were able to defeat vastly superior forces by applying the Principle of Momentum. The Principle of Momentum allows you to generate value that is authentic and valuable because it is created from the support of customers, partners, allies, friends, and individuals with a similar mind. The 10th Principle of the 25 Principles of Strategy teaches, above all, that creating and building momentum can be the deciding factor between winning and losing in a given situation.

25 Principles of Strategy

THE PRINCIPLE OF HIGHER GROUND

The 11th Principle of the 25 Principles of Strategy states that finding and holding higher ground can lead to winning. Higher ground should be viewed as a competitive advantage. Finding a competitive advantage is simple but to quote Carl Von Clausewitz "The simplest things are the most difficult". Finding a competitive advantage is a search that takes time and once found, it must be guarded, developed, and benefitted from. All leaders understand the importance of finding and owning a competitive advantage, but not all leaders are able to successfully source one. And even less are able to intelligently benefit from one. A competitive advantage cannot be forced but a competitive advantage can be discovered. Most competitive advantages are developed naturally or have existed without being exploited or used to any purpose. In

25 Principles of Strategy

order for a competitive advantage to be gained, the current situation should be analyzed for its benefits and dangers, strengths and weaknesses, and opportunities and traps. In a military conflict, the Principle of Higher Ground dictated that the army or force that held the higher ground, effectively held a competitive advantage that it could exploit. Castles were generally placed in difficult to reach places, whether near or on mountains, hills, or cliffs, in order to make its defense more secure. The cliffs of Scotland provided Scottish castles with maximum protection, increasing the chances for a defense against the English war machine. Moats around English castles were a competitive advantage as much as were mountains and mountainous terrain that made invasions of castles nearly impossible. Just like finding a competitive advantage in a situation, the locations of these castles had to be

25 Principles of Strategy

discovered. Competitive advantages in a situation, like the locations of impenetrable castles, must be discovered. The advantages cannot be forced or manufactured as the advantages will come about naturally by having the right conditions. The right conditions cannot be forced and that is where the Principle of Timing comes in to play. The 11th Principle of the 25 Principles of Strategy argues that finding and holding a competitive advantage can be the difference between winning and losing in a given situation.

PRINCIPLE OF TIMING

The 12th Principle of the 25 Principles of Strategy states that correct timing will lead to winning. Timing depends on conditions being met. If certain conditions are not met, your actions may be powerless, fruitless, or without result. Timing depends on all the right

25 Principles of Strategy

conditions existing and working in synchronicity to allow for your success in a given situation. Timing, also cannot be manufactured. The correct conditions must exist for your actions to find success. Even if a sequence of actions are completed with the hope of a certain outcome, if the timing is not right (the conditions to reach success are incomplete or missing), then the chances of success are greatly reduced and minimized. Some of the conditions in a situation may be influenced or altered, but the conditions to create the correct time cannot be manufactured.

"Water shapes its course according to the nature of the ground over which it flows; the soldier works out his victory in relation to the foe whom he is facing. Therefore, just as water retains no constant shape, so in warfare there are no constant conditions."

-Sun Tzu

25 Principles of Strategy

In order for there to success in timing, the correct conditions must not only exist, but they must also be able to be influenced. If you were to make a move prematurely this would sap your strengthen by depriving you of resources that can be used at a later stage. If you move too late, even expending extra resources may not be able to guarantee you any type of victory. The conditions must not only exist but must also be able to be shaped by your needs. Un-alterable conditions and rigid situations make for difficult situations for reaching success. Only by allowing the conditions to develop naturally and waiting patiently for the correct time to benefit from the conditions, is your future action guaranteed success. Conditions, as it has been stated previously, cannot be manufactured. Instead, the existence of the conditions are a pre-requisite to reaching success. The 12th Principle of the

25 Principles of Strategy

25 Principles of Strategy argues that timing is an essential element that can lead to winning in a given situation, but it is the existence of conditions that allow for the environment of success to develop. Sun Tzu in the Art of War stated that "The good fighters of old first put themselves beyond the possibility of defeat, and then waited for an opportunity of defeating the enemy."

PRINCIPLE OF DETACHMENT

The 13th principle of the 25 Principles of Strategy states detachment is an essential element of winning. Detachment signifies the action of moving away from something. Detachment is not retreat. Detachment is separation. This strategic separation is forced with the purpose of bringing about certain effects, least of all greater attraction. Attachment cannot exist without detachment

25 Principles of Strategy

and detachment cannot exist without attachment. For a scientist, detachment is essential because it allows for time away from the object of focus. This forced separation allows the mind to further contemplate what it has previously registered. Without detachment, this crucial period will be missed, denying the ability to develop a greater understanding of what has been learned. The greater the time of the detachment is, the greater the potential and probability that a deeper understanding will be gained. Detachment will allow you think over the situation and this will in turn give you various advantages that could not have been gained by not detaching. Constant attention may bring small gains in the beginning but the observer will eventually grow tired reducing their efficiency and productivity. Detachment allows for the re-growth of concentration and allows for re-focusing. In addition, detachment

25 Principles of Strategy

allows for, in military situations, time for re-supply of essential logistics that would allow them to continue their campaigns. Detachment creates time and space between you and the object of focus and it is this time and space that gives you a strategic advantage. Detachment is an important strategy that can be used to give you a key advantage precisely because the time and space separation empowers you. The 13th principle of the 25 Principles of Strategy argues that detachment is an essential strategy that can be the deciding factor between winning and losing in a given situation.

PRINCIPLE OF MANEUVER
The 14th principle of the 25 Principles of Strategy is the Principle of Maneuver. Maneuvering also known as mobility means to place or position yourself in a position where

25 Principles of Strategy

your strengths are leveraged against the opponent's weaknesses. The literal meaning of maneuver is "handiwork or manual labor used to defeat an opponent". Maneuver in the context of strategy refers to the movement of oneself vis-à-vis your opponent with the purpose of using your strength to overwhelm his weakness. Many military leaders such as Napoleon are famous for their extensive maneuvering techniques used on the battlefield. The Cuban Revolution under Fidel Castro and Che Guevara also owes its victory to the Principle of Maneuver. Che Guevara was a commander and strategic thinker that pioneered the use of maneuvering to defeat a stronger, well-armed opponent. In his 1961 book titled Guerrilla Warfare, Guevara said "The fundamental characteristic of a guerrilla band is mobility. This permits it in a few minutes to move far from a specific theater and

25 Principles of Strategy

in a few hours far even from the region, if that becomes necessary; permits it constantly to change front and avoid any type of encirclement. As the circumstances of the war require, the guerrilla band can dedicate itself exclusively to fleeing from an encirclement which is the enemy's only way of forcing the band into a decisive fight that could be unfavorable; it can also change the battle into a counter-encirclement (small bands of men are presumably surrounded by the enemy when suddenly the enemy is surrounded by stronger contingents; or men located in a safe place serve as a lure, leading to the encirclement and annihilation of the entire troops and supply of an attacking force). Characteristic of this war of mobility is the so-called minuet, named from the analogy with the dance; the guerrilla bands encircle an enemy position, an advancing column, for example; they encircle it

25 Principles of Strategy

completely from the four points of the compass, with five or six men in each place, far enough away to avoid being encircled themselves; the fight is started at any one of the points, and the army moves toward it; the guerrilla band then retreats, always maintaining visual contact, and initiates its attack from another point. The army will repeat its action and the guerrilla band the same. Thus, successively, it is possible to keep an enemy column immobilized, forcing it to expend large quantities of ammunition and weakening the morale of its troops without incurring great dangers." Positioning your strengths against your opponent's weaknesses will give you a strategic advantage that can be utilized for winning. The 14th principle of the 25 Principles of Strategy argues above all that maneuvering can be the difference between winning and losing in a situation.

25 Principles of Strategy

PRINCIPLE OF FLEXIBILITY

The 15th principle of the 25 Principles of Strategy teaches that flexibility can be the defining factor between winning and losing. Flexibility depends on being able to change tempo and adapt according to your opponent. Because all strategy is based on your opponent, your movements or actions should be based on your opponent. Water is the softest of substances, yet its strength is able to shape the land creating rivers and canyons where it flows. Water, although it is soft, is able to affect a much harder substance, that being rock. In conflict or competition, your opponent is not always predictable. Their actions may be purposefully formed to present non-predictability. If you attempt to present the same answer to every question you come across, you will be perplexed and confused because every question deserves its own

25 Principles of Strategy

unique answer. There is no way to create a solution that will fit every problem you come across. The way to be able to provide a solution to every new problem, is to create a unique solution for every new problem that you encounter. In a military conflict, resources are limited as are the manpower to direct. The Principle of Flexibility allows you to use economy of force by keeping a simple yet pliant form that can be changed according to the movements of your opponent. Sun Tzu in the Art of War says that "Water shapes its course according to the nature of the ground over which it flows; the soldier works out his victory in relation to the foe whom he is facing. Therefore, just as water retains no constant shape, so in warfare there are no constant conditions. He who can modify his tactics in relation to his opponent and thereby succeed in winning, may be called a heaven- born

25 Principles of Strategy

captain." The 15th principle of the 25 Principles of Strategy teaches that flexibility is an essential element that can be the defining factor between winning and losing.

PRINCIPLE OF DISRUPTION

The 16th principle of the 25 Principles of Strategy teaches that disrupting your opponent is an important part of winning. You may not be able to decisively defeat your opponent but you may be able to disrupt your opponent so that their plans do not come to fruition. Often in competition, a small move often equals zero or little gain. You may not be able to gain anything at all by competing against your opponent but you will be able to win by disrupting your opponent's plans. Disrupting your opponent's plans can be as simple as making moves that will not allow them to gain. In military conflicts, a hilltop was often sought

25 Principles of Strategy

to gain control of a battle. The troop that occupied the hilltop first would gain a major advantage in the battle. A military commander that orders placing obstacles for an enemy to occupy a hilltop would be considered the use of the Principle of Disruption. Although one troop is unable to occupy the hilltop, it actively prevents the other troop from occupying the hilltop in order to prevent any gain. This is a perfect example of the use of the Principle of Disruption. In Chess, if you occupy a position before your opponent, you are effectively disrupting your opponent by denying them the opportunity to occupy that position you are currently holding. Sun Tzu said "Whoever is first in the field and awaits the coming of the enemy, will be fresh for the fight; whoever is second in the field and has to hasten to battle will arrive exhausted. Therefore the clever

25 Principles of Strategy

combatant imposes his will on the enemy, but does not allow the enemy's will to be imposed on him. By holding out advantages to him, he can cause the enemy to approach of his own accord; or, by inflicting damage, he can make it impossible for the enemy to draw near. If the enemy is taking his ease, he can harass him." The 16th principle of the 25 Principles of Strategy teaches that disruption is an essential element in winning in a competition or conflict.

PRINCIPLE OF COMPARISON

The 17th principle of the 25 Principles of Strategy teaches that comparison is a key element that aids in your winning. Comparison means to make an honest and accurate survey of your opponent, including his strengths and weaknesses. Your opponent will reveal his patterns by his actions and it is his actions that provide the basis for comparison of his skills,

25 Principles of Strategy

abilities, and deficiencies. Sun Tzu in the Art of War said "Now the general who wins a battle makes many calculations in his temple ere the battle is fought. The general who loses a battle makes but few calculations beforehand. Thus do many calculations lead to victory, and few calculations to defeat: how much more no calculation at all! It is by attention to this point that I can foresee who is likely to win or lose." In applying the Principle of Comparison, you attempt to gauge the manpower of your opponent and by doing so you are able to better know them. Without comparison, you do not have a clear understanding of your own or of your opponent's strengths and weaknesses, putting you at a disadvantage. The Principle of Comparison is about better understanding of your opponent. If you know your opponent, you are able to have some level of confidence

25 Principles of Strategy

Che Guevara

about your plans becoming successful. If you do not know your opponent, you risk wasting valuable resources and losing resources due to

25 Principles of Strategy

lack of sufficient studying of the opponent. The Principle of Comparison allows you to draw comparisons so you understand where you are positioned (stronger or weaker) in regards to your capabilities. Comparison is a tool for wise leaders that understand that more knowledge about your opponent gives you a greater sense of security because you are able to shape your defenses to counter your opponent's strengths. The 17th principle of the 25 Principles of Strategy teaches above all that comparison is a key element to winning in competition.

PRINCIPLE OF DISCIPLINE

The 18th principle of the 25 Principles of Strategy teaches that discipline can be the deciding factor between winning and losing in a situation. Discipline means maintaining a standard level of cohesion that will allow you to achieve your objectives. Discipline is achieved

25 Principles of Strategy

by establishing the standards which you demand so there is no confusion as to your policies. Then punishments and rewards can be established according to the policies that have been announced beforehand. Discipline must be established first and loyalty must be built over time so that supporters could be gathered for achieving key objectives. Discipline is achieving by setting examples and maintaining order. Order is achieved through discipline and discipline is achieved by establishing policies that are known by all those affected by the policies. Discipline is not about maintaining a rigid or strict stance. Discipline is about setting standards and policies that will allow for the growth of skills and the utilization of capabilities. Discipline is a regime or laws that allow for objectives to be reached. If rigidity is a part of discipline then flexibility will become difficult. Discipline should

25 Principles of Strategy

be established through policies but it should be flexible enough so that rigidity does not become the standard. Discipline should be applied equally and discipline should be maintained by the equal application of rewards and punishments. The greatest military commanders were able to use a just system of rewards and punishments to push their forces to achieve extraordinary gains in battle. The Principle of Disciple argues for above establishing and announcing standards from which policies can be created and implement, for the establishment of cohesion. The 18th principle of the 25 Principles of Strategy, the Principle of Discipline, teaches that discipline is a key factor in the assistance of achieving a win in a competition.

25 Principles of Strategy

PRINCIPLE OF SURPRISE

The 19th principle of the 25 Principles of Strategy teaches that surprise is a key element in the assistance of achieving a win. Surprise depends on the concealment of information from your opponent, in regard to your actions, plans, and direction. If your opponent understands beforehand what you are going to do then your plans and your resources will be of little avail. What good is having more resources if your plans have already been revealed to your opponent? More resources and more manpower does not equate to victory if your ability to affect surprise has been compromised. Surprise will allow you to gain an important advantage in a competition and this is precisely the reason why you should refer to the Principle of Silence so that your ability to use the Principle of Surprise will not be denied. The Principle of Surprise has

25 Principles of Strategy

allowed many weaker military forces to defeat stronger and better well-armed opponents. Surprise gives you an advantage because your opponent is wholly unable to prepare themselves for your advance. The intimate details of your advance come as a surprise to your opponent because your opponent is unable to know when you will advance. The Principle of Surprise teaches that your opponent can gauge the time and place of your advance and this causes them to have to expend resources to defend all areas. This weakens your opponent and causes them to waste precious resources that could have been used for more viable purposes. Many military commanders have used the natural lay of the land as well as natural weather conditions like fog or storms, to utilize the Principle of Surprise. The Principle of Surprise can give an important strategic advantage because it

25 Principles of Strategy

allows for you concentrate your resources against weaker forces. The reason why you are able to do is because your opponent is unaware of where your advance will start. The 19th principle of the 25 Principles of Strategy teaches that surprise is a key deciding factor between achieving a win or a loss.

PRINCIPLE OF DECEPTION

The 20th principle of the 25 Principles of Strategy teaches that deception is an important element in achieving success. Deception in this context depends on the use of tactics to fool your enemy. Chinese military leaders were famous for lighting thousands of torches and placing them in trees, to create the illusion of a large army, in turn causing their opponent to flee. During World War II, Allied Forces used fake plastic tanks to create the illusion of an army to fool Axis forces. Deception also allows

25 Principles of Strategy

for the distribution of false information in order to fool your opponent as to your true intentions. This deception gives you a key tool that can be implemented in order to gain a strategic advantage. The application of the Principle of Deception involves the use of a ruse or lie to fool your opponent, causing them to make a mistake. The Principle of Deception is as much about putting your opponent in to an awkward position as it is about creating an opportunity. The opportunity is created by the mistake of your opponent. The mistake of your opponent comes about because of their incorrect perception of your actions. It is the deception that causes them to have a false perception. Deception creates opportunities, gives advantages, and allows for gains, if implemented and used correctly. Deception involves presenting a face that is the opposite of what the reality dictates. If your forces are

25 Principles of Strategy

outnumbered you can use ruses that will allow you to show that your forces are superior. If your resources are limited, you can use ruses to show that your resources are in surplus. Your opposition should not be made aware of the true reality of the situation because that will provide them with opportunities to exploit to your detriment. The 20th principle of the 25 Principles of Strategy teaches that deception is an essential element in a wise leader's strategy toolbox.

PRINCIPLE OF SPEED

The 21st principle of the 25 Principles of Strategy teaches that speed is a key factor that can lead to you winning in a competition or conflict. Speed depends on rapidity or the ability to maintain a high pace tempo. Speed has historically allowed weaker military forces to defeat stronger and larger armies. Sun Tzu

25 Principles of Strategy

in the Art of War stated that "Thus, though we have heard of stupid haste in war, cleverness has never been seen associated with long delays. There is no instance of a country having benefited from prolonged warfare. It is only one who is thoroughly acquainted with the evils of war that can thoroughly understand the profitable way of carrying it on." Speed brings conflicts or competitions to an end quickly, reducing the resources and manpower that is utilized. Slow campaigns can mean loss of resources and even loss of organization. By applying the Principle of Speed, military commanders have historically been able to maneuver past their opponents with minimal losses of resources. Rapidity is about bring the competition or conflict to a quick end by not allowing circumstances to affect a delay. The Principle of Speed allows for a culture of rapidity to develop and rapid plans to be

25 Principles of Strategy

created and implemented. Rapidity creates rigidity by limiting the amount of options available but also defines the options by the limitations. The limitations define the options available to be chosen rapidly because the options have been created beforehand and tested. Rapidity allows for bringing a competition or conflict to a speed end while limiting the amount of resources you will have expended to achieve your goals or task. The implementation of the Principle of Speed allows for the creation of opportunities that would not have been able without its implementation. In the Art of War, Sun Tzu states that "When a warlike prince attacks a powerful state, his generalship shows itself in preventing the concentration of the enemy's forces. He overawes his opponents, and their allies are prevented from joining against him." Sun Tzu is referring to the implementation of

25 Principles of Strategy

the Principle of Speed, which would allow one side to dominate another in a conflict. Speed not only creates key opportunities (that could not have been gained without speed) from which victory can be drawn from but also allows for one side of a conflict to overtake another through the sheer use of rapidity as a strategic advantage. The 21st principle of the 25 Principles of Strategy teaches that speed and creating a culture of rapidity is an essential element to victory.

PRINCIPLE OF YIELDING

The 22nd principle of the 25 Principles of Strategy teaches that yielding is an essential element for winning in a competition or conflict. Yielding means to "give way" in the face of the opponent. If the opponent is pushing you, yielding would allow you to move back and away from your opponent. Rather than meeting

25 Principles of Strategy

the force of your opponent directly, you would seek to yield to the force of your opponent, in effect luring them in. Yielding would give a key advantage to a weaker force that is facing a military force with superior numbers. By yielding, the weaker force will be able to draw in or lure the stronger force. Yielding allows for the creation of opportunities to apply greater strength to weaker less defended areas, giving the weaker force an advantage in a conflict or competition. Yielding is used by weaker forces in contrast to stronger forces that will advance almost hesitantly. The greater the yielding, the greater the opportunity for the weaker force to benefit. Stronger forces have no need to yield and this makes them both vulnerable as well as able to be lured in. Yielding means to not stop your opponent's intention. Sun Tzu in the Art of War stated that "At first, then, exhibit the coyness of a maiden, until the enemy gives

25 Principles of Strategy

you an opening; afterwards emulate the rapidity of a running hare, and it will be too late for the enemy to oppose you." Yielding means to continue in the direction of your opponent's intentions in order to control them. Yielding is not opposing your opponent but is it about conforming to the wishes of your opponent, in order to gain a strategic and/or tactical advantage over them. The 22nd principle of the 25 Principles of Strategy teaches that yielding is an essential factor to winning against a stronger opponent in a conflict or competition.

PRINCIPLE OF RESILIENCE

The 23rd principle of the 25 Principles of Strategy teaches that resilience is an essential element to winning in a conflict or competition. Resilience means to be able to recover quickly from a setback or a loss. The greatest military commanders have used this principle and have

25 Principles of Strategy

applied it to their forces in the face of defeat. Minor or even major setbacks are not a total loss. They may not even be a real loss. They may just be an opportunity for further reflection, contemplation, and planning. The Principle of Resilience dictates that major or minor setbacks are really a chance to re-group and to re-build strength, for the next advance. Resilience in the face of setbacks and difficulty requires a certain amount of discipline that must be gotten beforehand, so that the setbacks do not create apathy and indifference. Setbacks are transitory and not permanent but the application of the Principle of Resilience is constant. In the Art of War, Sun Tzu stated that "For it is the soldier's disposition to offer an obstinate resistance when surrounded, to fight hard when he cannot help himself, and to obey promptly when he has fallen into danger." Resilience means

25 Principles of Strategy

being able to stand up when you have been knocked down. Resilience means to be able to weather difficulties and problems so that you can rise above them. The greatest military commanders in history were able to recover from seemingly impossible odds and to reverse their situations, forcing them in to a win. But it is only by being able to withstand the various difficulties that will be presented that you will be able to recover from nearly un-fixable situations. The 23rd principle of the 25 Principles of Strategy teaches that resilience is a key factor that will lead to winning in a conflict or competition.

PRINCIPLE OF DEFENSES

The 24th principle of the 25 Principles of Strategy teaches that defense is the backbone and foundation of a strong offense. In the beginning of the establishment of the religion of

25 Principles of Strategy

Islam, the Muslims were outnumbered and under pressure of being slaughtered by the richer and more powerful pagans that ruled over Mecca and Medina in Saudi Arabia. Iranian military strategist Salman Farsi provided key military consulting to the Muslims and Muhammad, allowing them to defeat the stronger pagan armies headed by the merchants of Mecca. One of the tactics based on the Principle of Defenses that Salman Farsi introduced to the Muslims was the trench. The trench is a channel that is dug around a fort, castle, or building in order to stop cavalry and foot soldiers from accessing the walls during a siege. This essential yet simple military tactic was influenced by the Principle of Defenses. Sun Tzu stated in the Art of War that it is more important to focus on your weaknesses and seeing that your weak points are defended than to focus on weakening your enemy. If you

25 Principles of Strategy

are able to be in a position where you are completely defended, then offensive maneuvers become easier to implement. Although setting up defenses in various forms can be viewed as tactical actions, it is important to note that tactics are derived from the original strategy. The strategy of the Principle of Defenses argues for making yourself and/or your position invincible in order to never face defeat at the hands of your opponent. The Principle of Defenses ultimately argues for defensive postures over offensive postures. The Principle of Defenses calls for the implementation of tactics that will make your impervious to attack while providing you the opportunity or capability to enact offensive maneuvers. This principle that a strong defense will empower and strengthen you so that your offensive maneuvers will be more

25 Principles of Strategy

Miyamoto Musashi

25 Principles of Strategy

effective. Defense, in this principle, is more valued than offense. The 24th principle of the 25 Principles of Strategy argues that above all, defense is more important than offense for winning in a competition or conflict.

PRINCIPLE OF LEADERSHIP

The 25th principle of the 25 Principles of Strategy teaches that leadership has no friends and creates enemies. No one wants to see anyone in a place of a leadership when they themselves are not in that same position. Leadership breeds contempt, jealousy, envy, and hatred. People tend to dislike when a person is more knowledgeable than they are or if they are more knowing then they are. Leadership is lonely and has no friends because if a decision comes out correctly you will not be given credit for it and if the decision turns out badly you will be given the blame for

25 Principles of Strategy

Niccolo Machiavelli

it. That is why the Principle of Leadership
teaches that above all you must be thick
skinned and able to deal with criticism and

25 Principles of Strategy

sometimes rebellion. Criticism, when not constructive, is utterly useless and invaluable. Leadership empowers the leader to make decisions on behalf of supporters, but if the decision does not assist the supporters, the leader may come under scrutiny and face criticism. Criticism is good because it allows us to become better. When criticism is false, it does not assist in any way whatsoever. When criticism is heart sourced and true, it will allow you to become a better leader. Criticism is an opportunity for bettering ourselves and becoming more polished and more perfect in our work. Criticism, when done rightfully, should be rewarded and applauded rather than shunned. A leader is a leader because they set the direction. Leaders depend on the effectiveness of their operating system in order to ensure that they are able to achieve the goals or task which they set out to do. Leaders

25 Principles of Strategy

Chinese General Cao Cao

25 Principles of Strategy

will face opposition and commentary, but should be able to calmly and politely answer any and all questions addressed to him or her. Without leadership in everything, there may be confusion, chaos, anarchy, and disorganization. Leaders are able to unite and empower, motivate and inspire, and dictate and set the direction. The greatest leaders know when to delegate, when to manage, and when to be a visionary. If a household is considered a business and the head of the household is considered the leader, then it is the leader that is actively setting the way for the rest to follow. A great leader can lead his or her people to great achievements. A poor leader will weaken the household and may cause more problems than he or she is able to solve. The Principle of Leadership argues for single minded dedication to the goal or task without the regret that could result in apathy.

25 Principles of Strategy

Toyotomi Hideyoshi

25 Principles of Strategy

Leaders should be able to deal with apathetic individuals and prosper in the pressure of progress. The 25th principle of the 25 Principles of Strategy states that leaders should be powerful and not swerve in the face of opposition.

STRATEGIES ARE MANY

The numbers of strategies that are available to be used by a leader are many, but it is the actual implementation of the strategies that bear fruit. Strategy, is a means to an end, therefore the strategy or strategies chosen to be used should fit the actual scenario in which you are entering. There is no one strategy that will fit every situation because every situation is unique with its own conditions. Napoleon focused on maneuvering and flanking, while Sun Tzu argued for using a combination of strategies for winning. Cyrus the Great used

25 Principles of Strategy

Erwin Rommel is the most decorated military officer in history.

cooperation rather than competition to defeat his rivals. Carl Von Clausewitz argued for mobility and rapid deployment. Miyamoto Musashi mastered the Principle of Timing and

25 Principles of Strategy

Machiavelli argued that winning can be best achieved by "capturing" hearts and minds. All of their strategies are great and applicable, but it is important to note that each of their strategies came about because of conflict and war. Conflict and war, philosophically, is an environment where mistakes are not rewarded. In conflict, a single mistake may mean the loss of the battle or worse, the loss of the campaign. This is why Sun Tzu stated that the General or military leader holds the fate of his people in his hand. A wise military leader will be able to utilize strategies that will prevent the unnecessary loss of life, wasting of resources, and misuse of manpower. The greatest strategists like Sun Tzu are the ones that were able to achieve victory without allowing bloodshed to occur. The wisest military leaders are those that were able to take a castle or a city without having to lose humans in the

25 Principles of Strategy

process. Sun Tzu's entire philosophy rests around the premise that the highest form of the Art of War is being able to defeat your enemies or opponents without having to resort to violence. Western military strategists have been accused of using the Art of War without knowing, understanding, or implementing the way of peace, and their critics might not be wrong. High ranking American military personnel like General Colin Powell and General Norman Schwarzkopf have boasted of the use of the Art of War's principles of rapid deployment, mobility, maneuvering, and flanking without praising the highest objective of the Art of War, which is peace. The objective of the Art of War is peace not war. Violence is viewed (and should be viewed) as a last resort for a leader. The first and most agreeable first option is always dialogue, negotiation, and diplomacy. That is what separates the wise

25 Principles of Strategy

Salman Farsi was an Iranian military strategist

25 Principles of Strategy

and the un-wise leader. The wise leader will seek to win by cooperation and negotiation rather than through "gunboat diplomacy" and economic pressure. The wisest leader will win without expending any resources, firing a single shot, or having to engage in any minor or major conflict. The 25 Principles of Strategy argues for diagnosing the situation, formulating a strategy, and implementing it, in order to reach your objective(s). Although the strategies are various and many, the strategy that must be ultimately chosen is the one that allows you to reach the objective more effectively. Leadership is the intended product of good leader development systems. The definition of Leader development is: the deliberate, continuous, sequential, and progressive process, grounded in values that grows individuals into competent and confident leaders, capable of decisive action. Leader

25 Principles of Strategy

development is achieved through the lifelong synthesis of the knowledge, skills, and experiences gained through institutional training and education, organizational training, operational experience, and self-development. Leaders play the key role in leader development that ideally produces tactically and technically competent, confident, and adaptive leaders who act with boldness and initiative in dynamic, complex situations to execute mission type orders achieving the commander's intent and organizational goals.

25 Principles of Strategy

STRATEGY FORMULATION
The creation of a strategy includes the following steps:

DIAGNOSE
In the Diagnosis Stage, you research and analyze the existing conditions, stakeholders, and resources available to you and your opponent. You do a Situational Analysis and you view your own strengths and weaknesses as well as that of your opponent. Define the strategic objectives that must be reached.

FORMULATE

In the Formulation Stage, you choose the strategy or strategies to use to reach your goal or task. This gives you a clear set of recommendations to implement.

25 Principles of Strategy

IMPLEMENT

In the Implementation State you implement the recommendations that are necessary to reaching strategic objectives.

"In respect of military method, we have, firstly. Measurement; secondly. Estimation of quantity; thirdly. Calculation; fourthly. Balancing of chances; fifthly. Victory. Measurement owes its existence to Earth; Estimation of quantity to Measurement; Calculation to Estimation of quantity; Balancing of chances to Calculation; and Victory to Balancing of chances."
-Sun Tzu

The strategy that is created or selected is one that should be applicable and implementable. Not all strategies fit every situation and not all strategies are applicable during the confusion

25 Principles of Strategy

NATIONAL
STRATEGY

ECONOMIC	PSYCHO-LOGICAL	POLITICAL	MILITARY

of conflict. The best strategy is the one that is most applicable and allows the leader to reach his or her objective with the least utilization of resources. Strategies are condition based meaning that the existing conditions in the situation demand the creation of the strategy. Since most strategy is based on your opponent, when seeking to select or create a strategy, it is imperative that you choose a strategy than can actually be implemented.

25 Principles of Strategy

STRATEGIC

OPERATIONAL

TACTICAL

Strategy, as a means to an end, demands pragmatism and logical decision. There is no room for wishful thinking or resting your fate on hope. Strategy diagnosis, formulation, and implementation depend on *realpolitik* and

25 Principles of Strategy

pragmatic decision making, with the outcomes, benefits, and dangers having been weighed beforehand. Strategy can be viewed as the art and science of developing and employing instruments of national power in a synchronized and integrated fashion to achieve theater, national, and/or multinational objectives. Strategy can also be viewed as the means, ways, and ends to achieve objectives.

"Leaders have found greater fidelity and helpfulness in those whom, at the beginning of their reign, they have held in suspicion, than in those who at the outset have enjoyed their confidence."
-Niccola Machiavelli

25 Principles of Strategy

4 PRINCIPLES OF BARON JOMINI

1. To throw by strategic movements the mass of an army, successively, upon the decisive points of a theater of war, and also upon the communications of the enemy as much as possible without compromising one's own.

2. To maneuver to engage fractions of the hostile army with the bulk of one's forces.

3. On the battlefield, to throw the mass of the forces upon the decisive point, or upon that portion of the hostile line which it is of first importance to overthrow.

25 Principles of Strategy

George Washington defeated superior British forces in the American War of Independence.

4. To so arrange that these masses shall not only be thrown upon the decisive point, but that they shall engage at the proper time and with energy.

25 Principles of Strategy

THE ORDER OF STRATEGY

Vision

In this stage the objectives are defined that must be met. The Grand Objective as well as the strategic objectives needed to reach the Grand Objective is defined.

Strategy

The ways and means are defined.

Strategic Plan

The plan is created and distributed.

Implementation Plans

Implementation Plan A

Implementation Plan B

Implementation Plan C

Implementation Plan D

Implementation Plan E

Implementation Plan F

Implementation Plan G

25 Principles of Strategy

STRATEGIC APPRAISAL

1. Define Objectives

2. Determine interests

3. Determine Intensity of Interests

4. Assess Information

5. Determine Strategic Factors

6. Select Key Factors

7. Formulate Strategy

Strategic appraisal depends on an accurate and honest analysis of the situation and the factors involved in it.

25 Principles of Strategy

The U.S. Army War College defines the levels of strategy within the state as:

• National Security Strategy (also referred to as Grand Strategy and National Strategy).
The art and science of developing, applying and coordinating the instruments of national power (diplomatic, economic, military, and informational) to achieve objectives that contribute to national security.

• National Military Strategy. The art and science of distributing and applying military power to attain national objectives in peace and war.

• Theater Strategy. The art and science of developing integrated strategic concepts and courses of action directed toward securing the objectives of national and alliance

25 Principles of Strategy

or coalition security policy and strategy by the use of force, threatened use of force, or operations not involving the use of force within a theater.

STRATEGIC FACTORS

Information
Facts and data relating to any aspect of the strategic environment in regard to the interest(s), including both tangible and intangible attributes and knowledge; assumptions; relationships; and interaction.

Strategic Factors
The things that can potentially contribute or detract causally to the realization of the specified interests or other interests.

25 Principles of Strategy

Key Strategic Factors

Factors the strategist determines are at the crux of interaction within the environment that can or must be used, influenced or countered to advance or protect the specified interests.

STRATEGIC IMPORTANCES

Survival - If unfulfilled, will result in immediate massive destruction of one or more major aspects of the core national interests.

Vital - If unfulfilled, will have immediate consequence for core national interests.

Important - If unfulfilled, will result in damage that will eventually affect core national interests.

Peripheral - If unfulfilled, will result in damage that is unlikely to affect core national interests.

Source: National Security Policy and Strategy Academic Year 2007, pp. 106-108.

25 Principles of Strategy

STRATEGY EVALUATION

Applicable – Is the strategy or strategies applicable for reaching the objective or objectives?

Implementable – Is the strategy or strategies implementable? Can they objectives be achieved using the said strategies?

Feasible – Does the use of resources justify the objectives?

It is vital that you evaluate the strategy that you are developing and to ask the following questions so that you are assured that the strategy you are using is correct.

25 Principles of Strategy

STRATEGY GLOSSARY

Ceasefire – Cessation of hostilities.

Conflict – An economic, political, social, or military clash.

Competition – Strategic consideration that seeks rivalry and opposition rather than interdependence.

Cooperation – Strategic consideration that seeks alliances and interdependence rather than competition and rivalry.

Détente – A state of no peace and no war.

Diplomacy – Official communications between nations that is used for political purposes.

Ends – Objectives.

25 Principles of Strategy

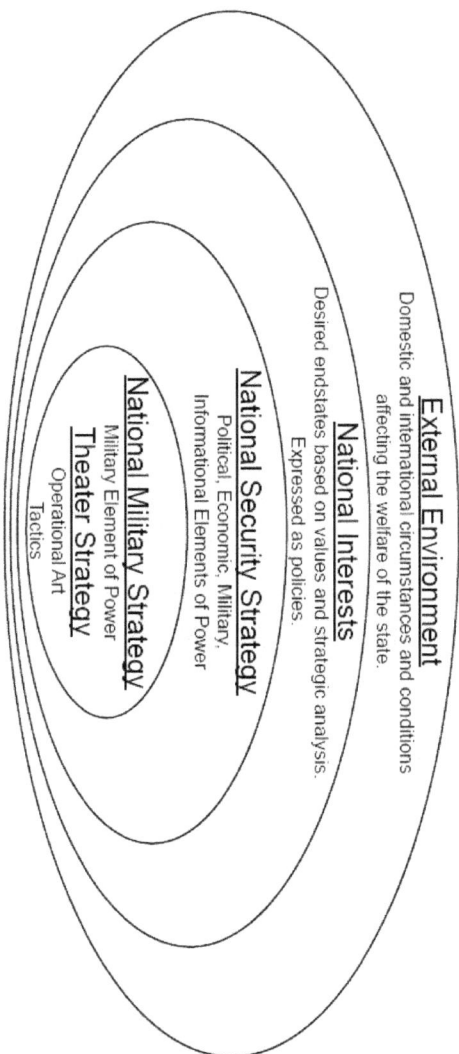

External Environment
Domestic and international circumstances and conditions affecting the welfare of the state.

National Interests
Desired endstates based on values and strategic analysis. Expressed as policies.

National Security Strategy
Political, Economic, Military, Informational Elements of Power

National Military Strategy
Military Element of Power

Theater Strategy
Operational Art
Tactics

25 Principles of Strategy

Flanking – Maneuver that concentrates superior forces against a weaker force.

Grand Strategy – Main strategy from which strategic objectives and implementation plans are derived.

Losing – Failing to meet objectives.

Luring – Tactic that draws the opponent in causing them to be ambushed.

M.A.D. – Mutually Assured Destruction argues that there is no winner in a nuclear conflict and that all parties are losers.

Maneuver – A tactic that gives you an advantage.

25 Principles of Strategy

Means – Resources available to reach objectives.

Mobility – Tactical movements designed to keep the opponent off balance and at a disadvantage.

Rapidity – Speed in deployment and implementation of strategies.

Scipio Africanus – Roman General and military strategist that defeated Hannibal in battle in the Second Punic War.

Strategic Advantage – An advantage that is gained and exploited in a competition or conflict.

25 Principles of Strategy

Strategic Analysis – Study of the situation, its conditions, problems/objectives, and resources needed to complete objective(s).

Strategic Objective – An objective that must be completed in order for the main objective or Grand Objective to be reached.

Strategy – Ways, Means, and Ends to an objective or objectives.

Sun Tzu – Chinese military strategist that pioneered and authored the Art of War.

Tactics – Actions that implement strategy.

Ways – Methods or tactics available to reach objectives.

Winning – Completing objectives.

25 Principles of Strategy

ACKNOWLEDGMENTS

Shervin Khoramianpour

California State University Dominguez Hills

25 Principles of Strategy

25 Principles of Strategy

SOCIAL MEDIA
Please support Kambiz Mostofizadeh by visiting his social media sites at:

Facebook.com/KambizMostofizadeh

Instagram.com/KambizMostofizadeh

Amazon.com/author/kambizmostofizadeh

kambizmostofizadeh.tumblr.com

kambizmostofizadeh.wordpress.com

kambizmostofizadeh.blogspot.com

https://www.linkedin.com/in/AuthorKambizMostofizadeh

Your support is **most appreciated**.

25 Principles of Strategy

NOTES

25 Principles of Strategy

NOTES

25 Principles of Strategy

NOTES

25 Principles of Strategy

NOTES

25 Principles of Strategy

NOTES

25 Principles of Strategy

NOTES

25 Principles of Strategy

NOTES

25 Principles of Strategy

NOTES

25 Principles of Strategy

NOTES

25 Principles of Strategy

NOTES

25 Principles of Strategy

NOTES

25 Principles of Strategy

NOTES

25 Principles of Strategy

NOTES

25 Principles of Strategy

NOTES

25 Principles of Strategy

NOTES

25 Principles of Strategy

NOTES

25 Principles of Strategy

NOTES

25 Principles of Strategy

NOTES

25 Principles of Strategy

NOTES

25 Principles of Strategy

NOTES

25 Principles of Strategy

NOTES

25 Principles of Strategy

NOTES

25 Principles of Strategy

NOTES

25 Principles of Strategy

NOTES

25 Principles of Strategy

NOTES

25 Principles of Strategy

NOTES

www.ingramcontent.com/pod-product-compliance
Lightning Source LLC
Chambersburg PA
CBHW071553040426
42452CB00008B/1156